AF316679

# Haunted Halloween History

E.V. Eklund

Published by E.V. Eklund
Seattle, WA


ISBN: 979-8-218-15013-6
Copyright © 2023



Author & Artist
E.V. Eklund

Halloween and its history have always held an intrigue for me, as I know it does for many people. Over the years, I have read numerous books and resources on the subject. The more I delved, the more I sought to seek answers to questions that arose.

Traditions, cultures, taboos, beliefs, religion, customs; all influence how we've evolved over the years, decades, and centuries. How we talk, dress, and come together to celebrate the holidays take bits and pieces from all over.

Many legends and folklore are told through poems and songs, so I thought this book fitting, as such, to be written in rhymic verse. The illustrations in this book were created and inspired by many vintage Halloween images. Each illustration is a reflection of the style to which the poem is based.

Perhaps you've always wondered why black cats are considered bad luck, or why kids go trick-or-treating...
Well, I hope this book sheds some light on the subject.

Dedicated to my family

# CONTENTS

# CREATURES & SYMBOLS



# LEGENDS & TALES



# BIBLIOGRAPHY

Traditions
&
History

# Go A-Souling

Go, go a-souling on All Souls' Day,
For those who passed this year, we do pray.
Traveling around from door to door,
Saying prayers for those who are no more.
A wish to the deceased in exchange for treats,
Thus began a practice of receiving sweets.
A day to look back on those who met demise,
A chant so they will never again come to rise.

While barmbrack in the oven bakes,
Children beg for bites of soul cakes.
Singing songs at night, outside in the street,
While kids see what goodies they have to eat.
Soon a new tradition begins to arise,
As mothers at home bake sweet apple pies.
A sack of fruits, nuts, and a loaf of bread,
For saying prayers regarding the dead.

Twisted and tweaked this religious day,
Hoping it will not lead you astray.
Such traditions fade and tales retold,
With new stories created out of the old.
Customs forgotten of long since past,
A telling of truths comes forth at last.
Trick-or-treating each year we persist,
A known custom we cannot resist.

# Guising

In the dark medieval times, way back when,
A time not dawned before the age of men,
Such a practice was forged from Allhallowtide,
To disguise and walk amongst those who had died.
Behind the ragged cloth and the horrid brown mask;
How did such a tradition begin you may ask?

The first of November did mark the harvest's end,
So believed the night before spirits would ascend.
To guise in costumes for the souls of the departed,
Such did it lead to the traditions getting started.
An evening for mischief making and play acting in the dark,
A festive occasion that would make its historical mark.

Guising was all but forgotten out east,
In Eire, guising traditions were deceased.
When the Irish came to New England, across the seas,
Other Samhain traditions were brought over to appease.
Games, praying, and communal feasting came along,
With tales of folklore and legend composed in song.

It's hard to say if these are the same customs of today,
That it evolved into our modern trick-or-treating, or so some say.
We like to think there is some link between the two,
Of the brown mask and the modern day dressed up fool.
Looking back on what our history may have to show,
To see how our customs might have begun long ago.

# Samhain & All Hallows' Eve

Turn back the clock to yesteryears of old,
To see what the past might have to unfold.
On All Hallows' Eve the moon shines out bright,
Lighting up the sky until dawn's first light.

Samhain marked the 'summer's end',[1]
As the winter season began to ascend.
Dark stories told around a bonfire,
With old verses sung out in choir.
Sacrifices and rituals made,
Bones as an offering to be paid.

With the two worlds at its most near,
The idea of spirits arising lead to fear.
That year in which a person dies,
Was believed their soul would come to rise.
So, to hide amongst the rising dead,
The idea of guising soon was spread.

Foreseeing what the future has to hold,
Wrapped up to fight against the night's cold.
From this pagan tradition of the dead,
A similar practice, later, was spread.
A Christian custom on All Hallows' Eve,
Show akin traits one would not believe.

Soon a practice of souling came around,
To pray for those no longer earthbound.
Offering chants, with songs to be blessed,
So that lost souls may be lain to rest.
Homemade sweets were then received,
In exchange for prayers for the grieved.

The history of these two customs may be sought,
Of whether the two are really related or not.
The answer may forever be a mystery,
But will always be etched in our history.


1 Pronounced 'Sow-wen'.

# Día de Muertos

Día de Muertos, The Day of Dead,
Many may mistake it as a day of dread.
However, this occasion is unlike any other,
Whether it's to honor a lost uncle or mother...
Is to bring about and to revive,
And reflect on those who were once alive.

At the stroke of midnight on All Hallows' Eve,
Brings about a celebration you would not believe!
Prayers are said for those who've passed,
Till second of November the occasion does last.
Reflecting on family members deceased,
And preparing a spread for a prestigious feast.

Marigolds and sweets are set to honor,
Used as offerings atop an altar.
On the ofrenda, photos are placed,
So one's family memories are not erased.
Sugar skulls, tamales, and sweet bread,
Made in memory of the dead.

Now the tradition has spread,
To observe The Day of the Dead.
So this festivity continues to bloom,
Dressing in paint and decorative costume.
Such an occasion is this,
That it is not one to miss!

DIA DE LOS MUERTOS

# All Saints' Day

On Nov. 1 Catholics are compelled,
In which a tradition is upheld...
To celebrate All Saints' Day.

A spiritual bond that is giving,
Between those in heaven and the living...
To honor all Saints.

A day to visit shrines and take care,
To give blessings and offer prayer...
Dedicated to all Saints.

# All Souls' Day

On Nov. 2 prayers are said,
To give blessings for the dead...
Called All Souls' Day.

For those of faith who had died,
But had not yet been purified...
So they may pass on into Heaven.

In cemeteries people embark,
To light candles in the dark...
So the deceased may find their way.

# Tombstones

Dating back to Celtic and Roman time,
Tombstones were associated with nighttime.

By the mid-seventeenth century they were found,
Commonly in churchyards and hollow ground.

By the Victorian era, they added more inscription,
Markers became more elaborate in their description.

In Mexico, on Día de los Muertos (or Day of the Dead),
Family would visit gravesites, bringing offerings of bread.

For most, graveyards are associated with fear,
In believing spirits returned this time of year.

# Halloween Hues

It was believed in the days of yore,
That such colors derive from Celtic lore.
With the year's harvest at an end,
Cover of night would quickly descend.

Dark is the eve in the absence of light,
Nothing to be seen but the mists of night.
Black as death, as the season dies,
Swiftly the summer meets its demise.

The change of the crops would soon turn,
As the previous season would adjourn.
Colors would alight in the gloomy days,
With reds and yellows shown ablaze.

Pumpkins ripened in the fall,
Laid with colors of orange for all.
As the foliage turned over a new leaf,
A new year begun was the belief.

# Haunted Houses

Here you were born, here they will mourn....
Where your memories and presence remain.


Nineteenth century London is where we begin,
  Where such attractions were made.
Displays created to entertain,
  With illusions to make you afraid.


Tussaud brought about the art,
  Making sculptures out of wax.
Molding death masks to shock,
  Who had fallen from the axe.


This eerie attraction got attention,
  Becoming popular far and wide.
Dubbed the "Chamber of Horrors",
  Leaving its viewers wide-eyed.


On All Hallows' Eve night,
  Vandalization would serge.
During the Great Depression,
  This is where an idea would emerge.


To prevent boys from damaging,
  And keeping them off the street,
Ghost houses were created,
  To scare them off their feet.

Soon it was commercialized,
  With more effects to scare.
Haunted houses became a hit,
  A new audience to ensnare.

Addressing houses with a history,
  A great structure to behold,
Such stories of ghosts and spirits,
  Were associated with places of old.

For a time, it was custom,
  For those who've just passed,
To be laid out in their home,
  Now a practice of the past.

The resting spot of the departed,
  It was only natural to believe,
That the spirit continued to reside,
  Giving a place for them to grieve.

Here is your home, here you will roam...
Where your memories and presence remain.

# The Corn Maze

We first glimpse at Labyrinths,
   Thousands of years before.
In the great land of Egypt,
   Entwined with tales of folklore.

Created once to enlighten,
   And not to bemuse.
Forming a single winding path,
   With only one way to choose.

Initially for processions,
   It symbolized the spiritual.
In the time of the Romans,
   It was also used as ritual.

Embellished from tile or mosaic,
   Designs were etched in the floor.
Found on walls and in churches,
   Forming ornate and elaborate décor.

Not until the Renaissance came,
   Were maze hedges brought about.
Creating quite a complex puzzle,
   With a series of paths branching out.

It wasn't until the year 1993,
  Where the idea was born,
In Annville, Pennsylvania,
  To make the first maze of corn.

Grown in popularity,
  They've become quite the craze.
Festive for the harvest season,
  Therein lies the story of the corn maze.

1993

# Cabbage Night

The night before Halloween,
Was known as Cabbage Night.[1]
Such mischief-making to be seen,
That rowdiness took flight.

Vandalism did stir,
Setting cabbages aflame.
Such tomfoolery did occur,
Treating it all like a game.

Rotten cabbages were collected,
And old vegetables they'd load.
At houses they were directed,
And thrown into the road.

A future to call upon,
Above your door you'd place.
Whomever the cabbage fell on,
Would be the one you'd embrace.

Such pranks are now fleeing,
And hijinks, tamed down.
Now pranks such as teepeeing,
Can be found around town.

1 Also known as Mischief Night, Goosey Night, or Gate Night.

# Bonfires

On the eve of Samhain, Celtic Druids believed,
That spirits returned to earth; this they perceived.
Marking the last day of summer, a new year to begin,
A boundary where living and dead were spread rather thin.
A reflection of the harvest season, long since gone,
Brought about in the absence of the dawn.


A light was brought forth, out in the night,
To create a blazing fire that burned out bright.
A 'bonefire' was created, to scare away,
All the evil spirits that arose that day.
Sacrificing animals and crops upon the kindle,
Ensured all unrestful souls would dwindle.


At the end of the bonfire, all would receive,
A cinder to light the darkness of that eve.
Placed in a turnip, in which to light their way,
In order to keep the arisen spirits at bay.
From this 'fire of bones', they would embrace,
To bring an ember home to their fireplace.

# Salem Witch Trials

Back in Colonial America,
A dark event took place.
Making its mark in history,
Such acts too horrid to face.

In Salem Village, Massachusetts,
Resided Puritans in the area.[1]
A colony with strong beliefs,
That became the fuel for mass hysteria.

Such views of religious fanaticism,
And that between good and evil,
That this led to fear and judgement,
With punishments that were medieval.

One January morn' in 1692,
Two girls were having a fit.[2]
They bellowed, howled, screamed,
They stomped, kicked, and hit.

A doctor soon approached,
And told them they were cursed,
Indicating that this was witchcraft;
This account was the first.

Two other girls fell sick,[3]
And panic started to take hold.
Rumors began to spread,
And accusations started to unfold.

A witch trial court was formed,
And in the spring, they pursued.
Suspects were questioned,
But beliefs over facts ensued.

Those that were brought forth,
Stated their plea in case,
Though it did no good,
For the court had no fact base.

Those labeled as a witch,
Hoped to be acquitted,
But were told to admit their guilt,
Or be tortured until they submitted.

At the base of Proctor's Ledge,
Bridget Bishop was the first.
With others soon to follow,
A fate to which they were cursed.

Fourteen women and five men hung,
While one was pressed to death.
"More weight" was his only reply,
As he took his last deep breath.[4]

Five more died of poor health,
From conditions in prison,
While others were not released,
Until the following season.

Many girls were incriminating,
With pins and needles of pain,
Never thinking it could be,
The result of bad grain.[5]

To the tree I do stand,
And join my siblings,
Hand in hand.

To the tree I will lay,
To save my soul,
To God I pray.

To the tree I go to sleep,
I pray my Lord,
My soul to keep.

1 First accusations first began in Salem Village. However, most of the witch trials took place in Salem Town.
2 Cousins Betty Parris and Abigail Williams, daughter and niece of Reverend Samuel Parris.
3 Ann Putnam and Elizabeth Hubbard.
4 Bridget Bishop, Sarah Good, Rebecca Nurse, Elizabeth Howe, Susannah Martin, Sarah Wildes, Rev. George Burroughs, George Jacobs Sr., Martha Carrier, John Proctor, John Willard, Martha Corey, Mary Eastey, Mary Parker, Alice Parker, Ann Pudeator, Wilmot Redd, Margaret Scott, Samuel Wardwell Sr. A man by the name of Giles Corey was the only one to be pressed to death.
5 Ergot, a type of fungus, that grows on rye.

Harvest
Treats

# Barmbrack

A future awaits ye', whate'er may betide,
Observe! A barmbrack with prizes inside.[1]

Receive a coin for wealth to behold,
For thy future will be prosperous with gold. 

Receive a green pea and you may dread,
For that year you shall remain unwed.

Receive a stick and it will bestow,
A life of marriage filled with woe.

Receive a ring and you'll be glad to hear,
For you shall be married within the year.

A bit of cloth is the bringer of bad luck,
Or a life of the poor shall you be stuck.

Read your fortune upon the plate,
To see what lies in your fate.

A future awaits ye', whate'er may betide,
Observe! A barmbrack with prizes inside.

1 Also known as 'fortune cake'.

# Soul Cakes

These sweets are supplied,
In batches during Allhallowtide.
For an act of virtue, a cross is laid,
To signify alms, to be displayed.

Amongst visitors they are given,
For the spirits that are driven,
To wander on the eve of that day.
May the dead find rest, they pray.

# On The Hearth

See lay, what your fortune may tell,
Cast upon the hearth, a lover's spell.

Commenced during the harvest night,
With divination given as your foresight.

Two chestnuts thrown upon the fireside,
Reveals the chance of the would-be-bride.

Note, what fortune telling may reveal,
If your marriage will be unjust or ideal.

Burning brightly, your chances fit,
Of a matrimony working to your benefit.

Should one nut jump towards the other soon,
Proposal will be yours before the next new moon.

# Apple Bobbing

An apple, an apple, dressed in red,
Celebrated on the feast of the dead.
Around and around, they sway to and fro,
Shimmering from the waters below.
The first to take a nab at an apple wins,
As the telling of this origin now begins.

A practice that goes way back,
Before witches dressed all in black.
A pail of water with apples afloat,
I recall the history, and I take note;
So let us start from way back hence,
Where this tale is about to commence.

The sole keeper of the orchard fruit trees,
As autumn brings about a crisp cool breeze.
A wood nymph of ancient Roman lore,
Pomona was the goddess at its core.
Now the arise of the new year,
As the winter season draws near.

A Cornucopia of apples brought for all,
In preparation for the end of the fall.
A look at what your future will hold,
With deep secrets awaiting to unfold.
The first to bite in the apple states clear,
Who will be yours to wed that year.

Once a divination, now just a game,
Understanding from whence it came.
Keeping the golden traditions alive,
Where they continue to flourish and thrive.
Many festivals continue to grow,
Brought forth from a long time ago.

GREETINGS
for HALLOWE'EN

# Cider

From the British Isles,
  The Romans did attest,
That cider came about,
  From apples being pressed.

A word coined by the Normans,
  Cider became one to favor,
For the taste reached far and wide,
  With folks taken with this flavor.

When colonies to America came,
  Their staple drink was beer,
But grains were hard to grow,
  Making their choice quite clear.

In season during harvest time,
  Its popularity only grew,
While during the winter months,
  This hardy drink lasted through.

Though different from today's,
  Where cider is more than sweet,
It's become a core choice,
  For the warm autumn treat!

# Popcorn Balls

At the turn of the last century,
They were a popular treat,
Found at every Halloween party,
They were a favorite sweet to eat.

Legend tells of the popcorn ball,
And how it came to be,
In the year of the striped weather,
In the plains of Nebraska, you'll see.

The hot sun shone on a corn field,
Then the weather turned to rain,
The field of corn started to pop,
And syrup washed from the sugarcane.

Flowing down the steep hill,
The syrup flowed into the popped corn,
Rolling, rolling, down the slope,
Soon the popcorn ball was born!

Though its popularity is waning,
Its taste is one to savor,
But for the present-day trick-or-treater,
It's store-bought candy they now favor.

# Candy Corn

Created by George Renniger in 1898,
It was a mellow cream of a sweet.
With the Goelitz Confectionary Company,[1]
This would become a hit of a treat.

Not until after World War II,
Was there an increase in demand.
Now marketed for Halloween,
Its popularity would soon expand.

Once named Chicken Feed,
Now Candy Corn it is known.
Even over a century later,
Interest and variety have grown.

1 Renamed and now known as Jelly Belly.

# Pan De Muerto

There are those who say that the origin of pan de muerto,[1]
Derived from the papalotlaxcalli, a butterfly seal stamped on dough.[2]

This tortilla was popular in the pre-Hispanic era long ago,
This theory has been supported by various institutions in Mexico.

However, research indicates that there is much to attribute to,
The Spanish and Catholic religion, from which their influence grew.

From Spain and nearby countries, with pan de ánimas was made a feast,[3]
For all saints and those departed, to honor and reflect on those deceased.

On All Souls' and All Saints' Day, these breads were placed on the grave,
Of a family member to show their love, an offering to which they gave.

Merged with Mexican customs, now a popular spread,
Placed on alters during commemoration of the Day of the Dead.

1 'Day of the Dead'.
2 'Butterfly Bread'.
3 'Bread of souls'.

Creatures
&
Symbols

# Classic Creatures

Dressing up as horrifying creatures,
A werewolf or witch with a warty nose.
Such monsters with grotesque features,
Such tales and legends arose.

Derived from stories and novels well known,
Others from past and ancient folklore.
Each creature with a story of its own,
Each with its own tale in store.

# Witches

Turn back to a chapter in dark history,
Many may wonder where witches derived.
Some believe such facts still remain a mystery,
Others wonder how such women survived.

Widows labeled as servants of Hell,
Though they would dispute.
They were locked away in a cell,
Those who were poor and destitute.

Such pets resided in a witch's habitat,
That superstitious folk started to believe,
That a familiar took the form of a dog or cat,
Working with her to corrupt and deceive.

Natural healers these old women may have been,
Practicing with herbs to treat an ailment or ache.
Appearing like sorcery, it was considered a sin,
They were then hanged or burned at the stake.

# Vampires

Vampires derived from a story of old,
    Based on an old true account.
A man whose life would be retold,
    And arise into the story of the Count.

Vlad the Impaler, so he was named,
    Reigned terror through his vengeful needs.
Killing and impaling enemies claimed,
    This was the source of his misdeeds.

A curdling tale came to arise,
    On what he used to feast.
Deaf he was to their pleading cries,
    As he drank the blood of the deceased.

Later was written in Victorian time,
    The novel 'Dracula' by Bram Stoker.
A story to be recited at bedtime,
    That was anything but mediocre.

Other gruesome events of yore,
    To explain such diseases unforgiving.
Stories that arose from Slavic folklore,
    Of the dead that feasted on the living.

So intertwined became these tales,
    That have given shape to the undead.
With vivid imagery in such details,
    That would fill your heart with dread.

# Werewolves

Many origins of the werewolf have been told,
  Throughout different cultures in time.
Some dating back to the ages of old,
  Filled with punishment and crime.

The earliest known man-to-wolf accord,
  Arose from the Middle-East.
From Mesopotamia the text on record,
  Told of a man changing into such a beast.[1]

The fables of monsters would increase,
  Tales from historic times formed.
Like the Legend of Lycaon from Greece,
  From which men to wolves transformed.

Other ancient stories of yore,
  Such as the Volsunga Saga of old,
Came from a Nordic folklore,
  Which spoke of magic wolf skins to behold.

Legends of the werwulf spread,
  From Europe in the Middle Ages. [2]
Accusations of lycanthropy and bloodshed,[3]
  Written down in the history pages.

Overtime these tales would appear,
  In Gothic horror fiction.
Novels written to instill fear,
  Leading to a new craze addiction.

Werewolf fables have been found,
    Such Native American tales born,
Of how a spirit would be bound,
    If from an animal, it was torn.

Accounts over the many years,
    Formed today's guise we now recognize.
Creating intrigue alongside our fears,
    Should a full moon come to rise.

As a man to wolf transforms,
    Only by a silver bullet can he be slain.
Tales written as the mythology forms,
    Bringing an end to the bearer's pain.

1 Referring to the story Epic of Gilgamesh.
2 Werwulf - Old English 'wer'-man and 'wulf' wolf.
3 Lycanthropy - supernatural ability for a person to shapeshift into a wolf.

# Ghosts

Since the dawn of man,
   Such beliefs became ingrained.
The idea of ghosts first began,
   To explain the unexplained.

In the Greek and Roman age,
   To keep the spirits content,
The living would engage,
   To make sure offerings were sent.

In China, ghosts crave the same,
   As they did when they were living.
Money tossed upon the flame,
   So the spirits weren't unforgiving.

To not appease the dead,
   Might provoke them to rage.
Ill luck may come to spread,
   As quick as the turn of a page.

Some believe spirits would remain,
   Should their life end in strife.
Things that caused anger or great pain,
   Would have them stuck in the afterlife.

Others had such devotion,
   Feeling loss and broken hearted,
They would entertain the notion,
   That the dead never truly departed.

# Mummies

In ancient times the Egyptians believed,
  In the preservation of life after death.
For this is what they perceived,
  For those who took their very last breath.

For the deceased, goods were buried,
  In secret chambers for safe keep.
In the darkness they were carried,
  Hidden treasures of the deep.

Disturbing the tomb of the dead,
  Such misfortune is said to ensue...
To which ill fate would be spread,
  The folks thought this to be true.

An idea of the mummy's curse was laid,
  Along the Nile's ancient land.
Such myths of crypts were portrayed,
  Of those buried beneath the sand.

# Demons

Since the dawn of theology they dwell,
  The stories of demons, they creep.
Arising from the Gates of Hell,
  In the darkness of your sleep.

During Samhain, at harvest end,
  A barrier between two worlds were broken.
From there, demons would ascend,
  Such beliefs in stories were spoken.

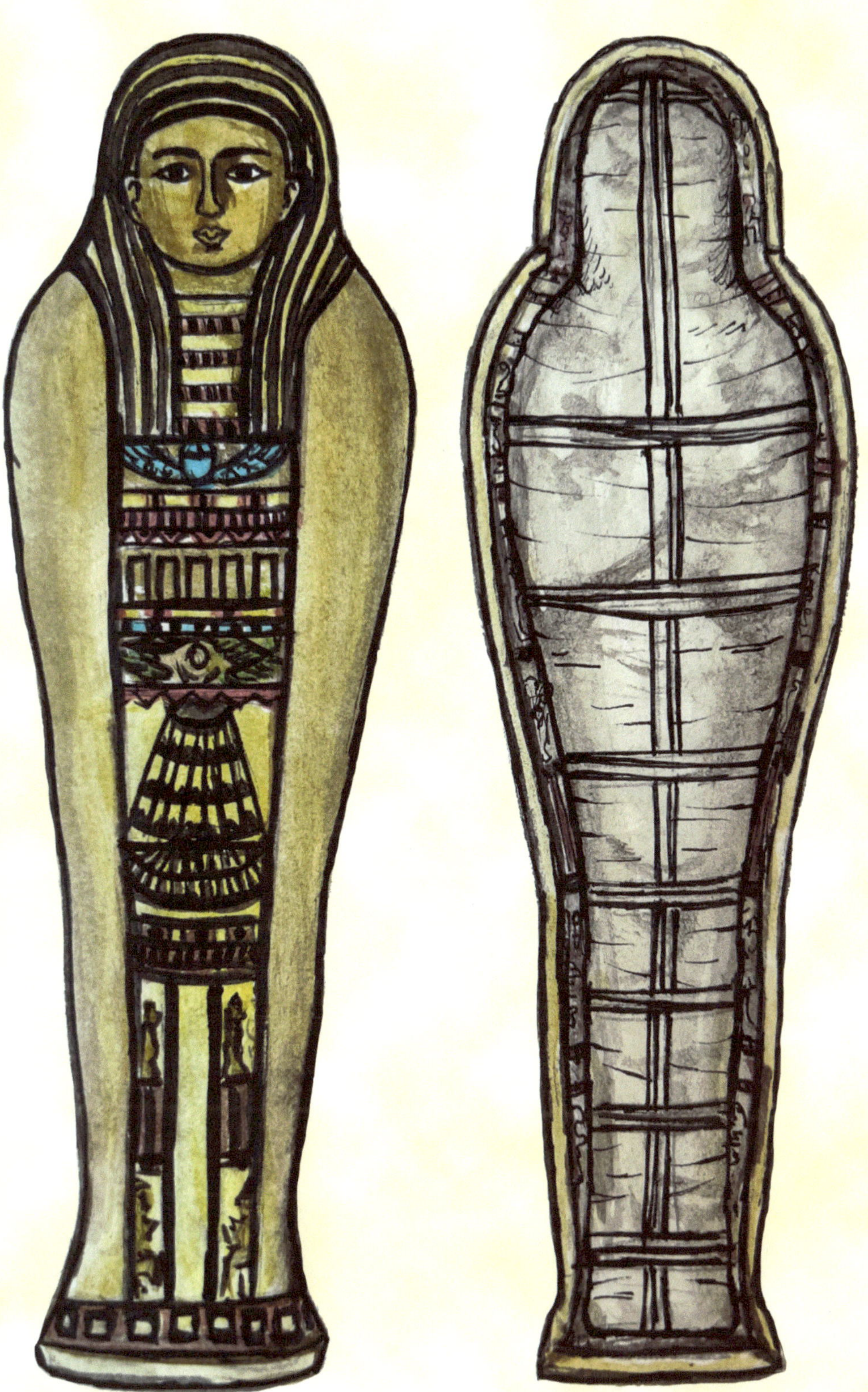

# Zombies

In Haiti...
Before the act of abolition,
   Such ideas began to take shape.
Under such brutal a condition,
   Slaves sought a way to escape.

For....
The hostile conditions they faced,
   Escape through suicide they sought.
Though they would be disgraced,
   It was the only way not to be caught.

However...
Taking your life was perceived,
   In losing one's control,
That they strongly believed,
   So trapped would be your soul.

For...
In taking one's own life,
   You would arise from your bed,
Cursed with an existence of strife,
   Not quite alive and not quite dead.

So...
It arose, these tales of lore,
   Of those of the undead.
Adding to it, flesh eating gore,
   Such did the stories spread.

# Skeletons

A festival Druids first began,
One would require,
Scarifies of animal and man,
To be tossed in a bonfire.

Bones would be burnt away,
As offerings to the dead.
To keep such demons at bay,
So the spirits may be fed.

Looking back through early pages,
Images of skeletons are found.
In scriptures during the Middle Ages,
As in death, they were bound.

Such readers may be perplexed,
To see these at first glance.
So described in the text,
To behold skeletons in a dance.

After the Black Death was gone,
People no longer would shun,
And instead faced death head on,
For Death waited for no one.

The human skull would turn into,
A symbol in early Christian scripts.
This death icon spread and grew,
Now displayed on graves and in crypts.

# Familiars

## Bats

In Celtic times, at harvest end,
   Bonfires were lit in the night.
Winged creatures would descend,
   Attracted by the light...
     Seen as bad spirits returning to earth.

Tales of vampire bats would appear,
   By the Spanish it was brought.
Stories from the New World came fear,
   Filling folks with such fraught...
     With stories of blood sucking demons.

Such frightful ideas were embraced,
   When the novel Dracula was released.
Such was the story based,
   About a wicked horrid beast...
     When vampires turned into bats.

## Toads

Changes in modification,
   Bringers of good luck to Wiccan.
Symbols of regeneration,
   Either to heal or to sicken...
     Kept as pets to witches.

# Spiders

Creepy and crawly in the dark,
   Found in dungeons and in caves.
Spiders may have made their mark,
   Being found amongst the graves...
      Seen as evil companions to witches.

Creating its home in plain sight,
   In a corner or shady spot.
Making cobwebs in the night,
   In hopes for flies to be caught...
      An icon for haunted Halloween houses.

# Ravens

In the darkness they take flight,
   The sky filled with their cries.
Gliding silently through the night,
   As they keep watch with their beady eyes...
      A messenger for the wicked.

Viewed as secretive and nimble,
   But the smartest of all birds.
Represented as an ominous symbol,
   Using different caws as words...
      Its call believed to be an omen of death.

# Rats

Transporting illness across towns,
    With fleas upon their backs.
Covering vast city grounds,
    Traveling in massive packs....
        Spreaders of the Bubonic plague.

Gruesome street dwellers,
    Fond of rotten food and cheese.
Found in sewers and in cellars,
    Carriers of sickness and disease...
        Seen as the bringers of death.

# Serpents

A mythological symbol of old,
    Shedding its skin to transform.
The ouroboros it is told,
    Means the renewal of life in its form...
        A symbol of modern medicine.[1]

However, they are not revered,
    And instead viewed as vile.
The snake is rather feared,
    For a strike can be hostile...
        With a bite poisonous.

1 Ouroboros - a serpent eating its own tail.

# Owls

This predator made itself appear,
   Only in the darkness of the night.
Making it an element of fear,
   An inhabitant of twilight...
      Becoming an air of mystery and suspense.

So believed medieval men,
   When you heard an owl cry,
Was regarded as a bad omen,
   Meaning you would soon die...
      A messenger for sorcerers and witches.

A nocturnal bird with such features,
   Moving their head clear around.
Seen as dark creatures,
   Who are not earthbound...
      Associated with All Hallows' Eve.

# Goats

A familiar that likes to revel,
   Set with square pupil eyes.
With horns like that of the Devil,
   A demon spirit in disguise...
      The embodiment of Satan.

# Black Cats

So where did the origin of black cats come to be?
Come sit and listen, and you will come to see,
That these 'tails' of cats are nothing but a tall tale,
So may this poem be a lesson at your avail.

From culture to culture, folklore does vary,
Some of it good fortune, while others, rather scary.
In Scotland, a black cat meant prosperity,
Upon arriving at your home, I say, for clarity.

In Britain, if along your path they'd stroll,
Are thought to bring good luck to the soul.
In Japan, black cats are thought to bring about health,
For others, it's a sign of good fortune and wealth.

Wives of fishermen would keep black cats at home,
While their husbands around the world would roam.
This would ensure the men's safe return,
And would ease their tension and concern.

Sailors of ships would take black cats aboard.
Soon these 'sail cats' were rather expensive to afford.
They would ensure fair weather and protection at sea,
These black cats were nothing but good you see.

However, in Europe, when the Dark Ages came,
A history of sickness, of famine, and flame;
Such horrid ideas they began to embrace,
With witch hunts becoming commonplace.

Such beliefs that arose were medieval;
To believe that solitary women were evil.
Those that were foul, desolate, and not rich,
Were labeled to that of the vile witch.

Seen as a companion for the lonely lady,
Black cats were viewed as rather shady.
Though such folks had household pets,
Many people accused, holding no regrets.

That such, should a witch be set ablaze,
So much their companions; so was their ways.
Many harmless pets put to their doom,
It did not cease but all too soon.

Black cats were regarded with superstition,
Being in line with the sorcery of a magician.
Such deceitful myths and fables had begun,
Claiming black cats were unholy and pagan.

False convictions continued to infest,
When Separatists made their way out west.
Believing such sinners must have been forsaken,
Further innocent lives were bound to be taken.

Such to their religion they felt an attack,
An anarchism tied with the color black.
The fear of these creatures greatly grew,
With misfortune being associated with this hue.

So the black cat was marked as bad luck,
An idea, that over time, went amok.
Such dangerous beliefs can have dire affect,
When labeling an object or certain subject.

Whatever your views of this mysterious cat,
I know where my judgment lies regarding that.
A cat is a cat, and if it's nice to you,
You can simply be nice to the black cat too.

By the
Moon

# Scarecrow

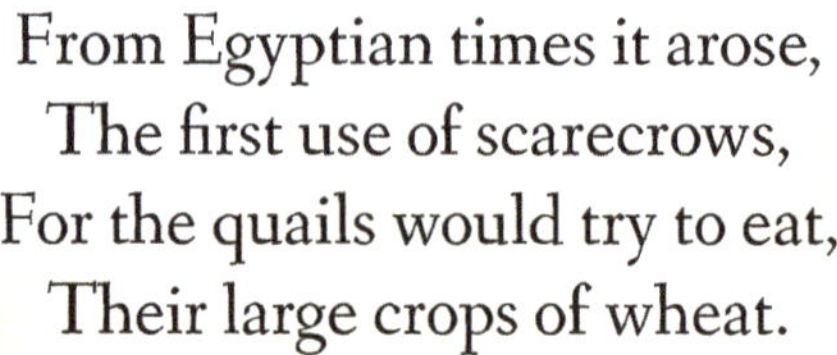

Found in pockets all around,
A practice set in the ground,
To keep birds, like the crow,
Away from fields long ago.

From Egyptian times it arose,
The first use of scarecrows,
For the quails would try to eat,
Their large crops of wheat.

The ancient Greeks erected,
Scarecrows that protected,
The fields over which they stood,
Carved from a stump of wood.

In Japan, they would shape,
A Kakashi to drape,[1]
Dawned with bells as a device,
To defend their fields of rice.

The New World settlers sought,
Same practices for their plot.
A scarecrow posted in the yard,
A field protector in which to guard.

Used during the harvest season,
Mischief boys would find a reason,
To pull pranks on a dare,
To use these figures at night to scare.

1 Meaning "scarecrow", with literal translation meaning
"something stinky", smelling hideously awful.

# Fortune-Telling & Divination

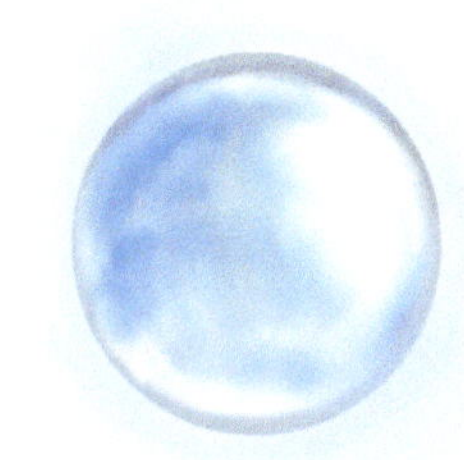

At the end of the harvest season,
When the two worlds are near,
The dead walk the earth,
And spirits soon appear.

This was a time to call upon,
The spirits for a request,
To see into their futures,
Such wishes they expressed.

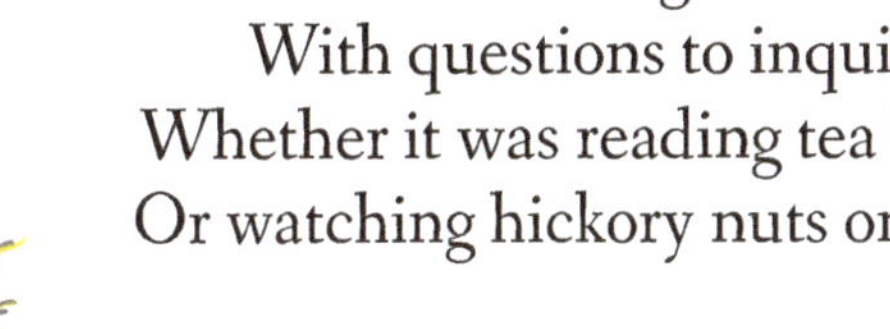

Fortune-telling amused,
With questions to inquire,
Whether it was reading tea leaves,
Or watching hickory nuts on a fire.

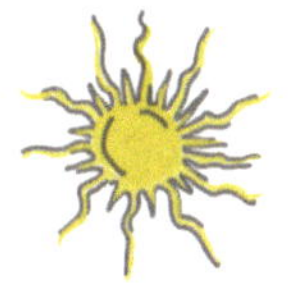

Reading one's palm,
To learn about your life,
Whether it was to be joyous,
Or filled with utter strife.

During the Enlightenment,
Tarot cards were first used,
For interpretating divination,
A practiced that thrilled and amused.

In 1890s, a board came out,
In order to communicate,
To the spirits beyond, [1]
And ask of it your fate.

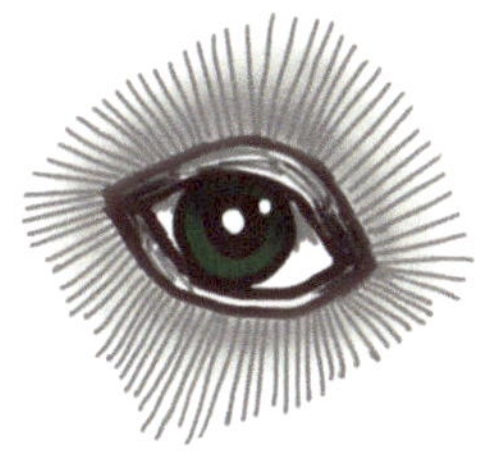

Many games were played,
What would you believe,
Interpreting a bite from an apple,
On All Hallows' Eve.

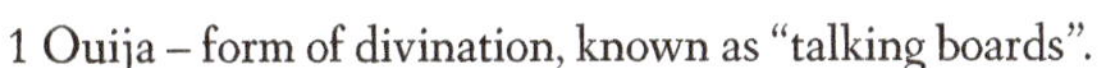

1 Ouija – form of divination, known as "talking boards".

# Witches' Hat

Many origins are debated,
On where this symbol originated...
Of the tall black conical hat.

Near China, mummies were found,
Upon their head they were crowned...
Wearing tall pointed hats.

Similar, with a brim that was flat,
And tall, like the German golden hat...
Used by priests during the Bronze Age.

Perhaps the witches' hat was inspired,
From the Judenhat, that was required...
To be worn as a marker long ago.

However, these seemed more based,
On ideas that are misplaced...
Concerning men and sorcery.

Since the late medieval ages,
Images have been found in the pages...
Of women and their dealings with the Devil.

The Age of Enlightenment saw,[1]
Figures one would carve and draw...
Of a witch with a pointy black hat.

The closest theory to attest,
And be authenticated at best...
Comes from the Quakers style of dress.

Their religion they embraced,
But such prejudice they faced...
With Anti-Quakers accusing with speculation.

Conical black hats they displayed,
A look that only helped to aid...
Negative connotation with witches.

1 Also known as the Age of Reason from late
17th century through early 19th century.

# Broomstick

To clear away negative energy,
Before a ritual it was believed,
One should sweep with a broom,
This was how it was achieved.

These views were forgotten,
Replaced with the misconception,
Of dealings with the Devil,
And his ways of deception.

Flying ointments were made,
That granted the gift of flight.
Upon her broom she would soar,
In the darkness of the night.

From poisonous plants they brewed,
Such balms put one in a trance,
Giving off strong hallucinations,
On a broomstick she'd dance.

# Cauldrons

The cauldron is a symbol,
    Seen throughout our history,
With a variety of meanings,
    Giving it an air of mystery.

There is a Pagan folklore,
    Dated many centuries ago,
That new souls would enter,
    And out, old souls would flow.

The Celts believed the cauldron,
    Is where all life originated,
And all would return once more,
    From whence they were created.

The cauldron was beheld,
    As a symbol of the womb,
A protected place to grow,
    In which new life would bloom.

A witch brewing potions,
    Soon became viewed,
From the old lady cooking,
    Over a fire preparing food.

# Legends & Tales

XLI
SAENS
1860-192[illegible]

# Danse Macabre

*Inspired by Danse Macabre by French Poet Henri Cazalis and composer Saint-Saens Op. 40*

Ding

Ding

Ding

Ding

Ding

Ding

Ding

Ding

Ding

Ding

Ding

Ding

Tik, Tik, Tik,
Death comes to rise, oh what a sight,
As the chimes call out at the stroke of midnight.
Striking a tune on his rustic violin,
Playing the dance of death whilst holding a grin.

Tap, Tap, Tap,
Tapping his sharp heel on a gray tomb,
While skeletons around him start to loom.
The bitter wind whistles in the cold breeze,
Eerie moans echo through the linden trees.

II. LV
JOHNSN

Clack, Clack, Clack,
Skeletons canter and caper in their shrouds,
As the moon breaks out through the clouds.

Clink, Clink, Clink,
Prancing and frolicing, they move to and fro,
As the bonfire gives off a charring glow.
A cloaked couple sits upon the fen,
Taking in the lost delights of the glen.

Rap, Rap, Rap,
Death continues to play,
Relentless 'til the break of day.

A veil falls, the dancer stands bare,
Her partner amorously grasps her with care.
A past baronness, once a lady fair;
Her skin, once luminous, shows signs of wear.
Her dauntless gallant, poised grand,
Is nothing more than a poor field hand.

Dismay! She would not forgo,
For what the rustic had to bestow.

Tick, Tick, Tick,
What a tune!
All dance in cirlces under the moon.

Click, Click, Click,
There in the crowd dances the king,
Amonst the peasants, round in a ring.

But Still! Suddenly they leave the dance,
The crowd pushes forward in advance.
They flee away, to their graves they crawl,
Just as the cock lets out its morning call.
Oh, what an alluring night to ensue,
As we bid the danse macabre ado!

# The Legend of Stingy Jack

Jack the Smith was a known drunkard and local chum.
He was a trickster, swindler, and low sod scum.
He would travel from pub to pub, around every night,
Drinking away, holding no grudge or any plight.

One gloomy night the Devil heard of his deceitful tricks,
And made a mind to go upstairs, with lit candle wicks.
He learned of Jack the Smith's vile reputation,
And took it upon himself to learn of his location.

He sat along the cobblestone path, looking for Drunk Jack,
Waiting in the chilled night, for the right course of attack.
As Jack turned the corner, a flask in his clammy hand,
The Devil came forward to test the inebriated man.

He stood there staring with a grimace on his face,
Jack knew this was one deal he could not out chase.
"You've been dishonest in your fraudulent ways,
You will go down below till the end of your days."

Stingy Jack looked on over, turning round to say,
"You may take me below, before the end of the day...
However, I request from you just one thing...
To lift my spirits, a swig of a mug to cling."

"A round of warm drinks of foaming good ale,
This I ask, before I'm made to set sail."
The Devil agreed, thinking nothing more of this request,
Walking alongside, treating him as his formal guest.

Round after round, drinks emptied, once filled to the brim,
The Devil waited patiently to what would soon belong to him.
Jacked turned with a grin, requesting the Devil to pay,
As he asked, there was, in his voice, a hint of betray.

"To pay for these hardy drinks, if you could, just for me,
Transform into a sixpence, what a thing that would be!"
The Devil saw no harm in his last request,
Knowing soon, all worries would be cast off his chest.

Jack held the silver coin in the palm of his hand,
Grimacing as he hatched up a scheme of a plan.
For within his coat pocket held a crucifix cross,
There, the silver coin, did he toss.

There, the poor Devil was stuck for good,
As Jack went out, pulling up his hood,
He spoke, "A pack I'll agree upon, only if you would..."
As the transmogrified Devil in his pocket stood.

Jack demanded in exchange for the Devil to be let free,
His soul not to be claimed for another ten years was his plea.
The Devil had no choice but to grant his behest,
Only in his best interest did he gift this request.

Ten years passed since the crook deal was made,
Where the promises between two lads were laid.
Returning once more, the Devil did come,
To claim the life of the forgotten son.

Jack agreed to accompany him down below,
As the eve of that night gave out a soft glow.
"But", queried Jack, "before I'm to depart to my grave,
There is but one last request to which I deeply crave."

"I am starving for just one apple on that tree,
If you could just go up top and fetch it for me."
The Devil saw no harm and started to climb the branch,
While Stingy Jack saw this as his one and only chance.

He went over to the bottom of that tree and started to carve,
A cross in the bark, making the Devil eternally barred.
Entrapped once again, the Devil demanded his release,
Shouting that this trickery of Jack's must cease!

An agreement was struck upon one last time,
Before the midnight clock gave out its last chime.
Jack's soul was never to be taken down to Hell,
Where corpses with tortured souls do dwell.

Over time, drink and instability lead to Jack's end,
With bitter death waiting for him just around the bend.
As he prepared to enter Heaven he was stopped by St. Peter,
Stating to Jack, "You were nothing more than a spiteful cheater."

"You drank, manipulated, deceived, and tricked,
Such lies on others you would inflict.
Now you will be cast out from paradise above,
For your doings have shown what you're really made of."

Unable to enter Heaven, he embarked to Hell below,
Begging to enter, his heart filled with grief and woe.
The Devil, having made a sealed pack,
Was not permitted to take Jack back.

To warn all others, to Jack he gave an ember,
Before the start of the harvest in November.
The fire from below, gleaming into the night,
Giving out in the dark, a strong lit light.

In a hollowed turnip, the beacon was placed inside,
As he reflected on those to whom he swindled and lied.
Forever trapped as a dweller in the secluded netherworld,
Eternally caught between two places to which he was hurled.

With only a glow of light as his side,
He wanders in darkness at his own stride.
Roaming in search of eternal rest,
Hoping to reach the end of his quest.

Legend has been told and a tale has been strung,
Of Jack of the Lantern and his trickster fun.
Still, he continues to wander on All Hallows' Eve,
Looking for drunk and foolish men to deceive.

Now in memory of Stingy Jack,
We cannot help but take a look back,
Of the legendary tale of that trickster man,
Proving misdeeds never work out according to plan.

Now on Halloween we keep our jack-o'-lanterns lit bright,
To keep away the darkness that comes for us at night.

# The Legend of Sleepy Hollow

*From 'The Legend of Sleepy Hollow' by Washington Irving, retold in poetic verse*

Looking back to a dark chapter in American history,
There lies a legend whose ending remains a mystery.
In New England there lies on down,
A quiet place just north of Tarrytown.
Alongside the Hudson, in a rural port within a glen,
Resided Dutch settlers way back when.
Beyond the rolling hills, you will come to see,
This secluded village enclosed in tranquility.
A long excursion for one to follow,
There, to the valley of Sleepy Hollow.

In this drowsy town, lingering by the river,
Lies stories that would make your bones quiver.
A dreamy place with a haunting atmosphere,
Where such legends have formed out of fear.
Inhabitants spoke in severe admonition,
Of ominous spots and twilight superstition.
Strange sites dwell along bewitching trails;
Such were the sayings in their local tales.
But never as notorious a tale would follow,
As that of the Headless Horseman of Sleepy Hollow.

So, it is told that during the Revolutionary War,
Where battles were fought with great valor,
A cannon ball struck a trooper with a blow,
In the outskirts of the Hollow long ago.
Beneath the churchyard the body was laid to rest,
Though his headless spirit was said to manifest.
In the gloom of midnight, he is said to ride,
In search of his head since the night he died.
Apparitions of a figure on horseback without a head,
Devised this story of the Hessian long since dead.

Now to turn our attention thirty years hence,
From this time to a remote age, I will commence.
In concerning a lean, lanky scarecrow of a lad;
His garments hung loose, appearing ill clad.
Donning a hooked nose, accompanied by vast ears,
He looked rather odd amongst his fellow peers.
So, from Connecticut came the new schoolmaster,
Unbeknownst of his approaching disaster.
A fellow by the name of Ichabod Crane,
Soon arrived within the Headless Horseman's domain.

Within a small structure that stood on the edge of a hill,
Laid silence, except by the sound of a scribbling quill.
Crane sat, his tall frame crouched over a wooden stool,
There, to scholar the young pupils in the school.
As the light shone through, and the sun came alive,
The pupils' voices arose like that of a beehive.
Mr. Crane was strict, but just, in his manners and ways,
Disciplining the bad and supplying the good with praise.
Often in holiday he would partake to accompany,
Students home to meet their pretty sisters for company.

Ichabod was housed in the homes of children he taught,
Along with daily bread, to which he was brought.
However, his appetite was grossly immense,
And he hardly considered this any sort of paid expense.
Evenings were spent in the company of old wives,
As they gossiped about their daily lives.
By the fire, they would work, spinning a row,
As the hearth let out a warm orange glow.
The apples roasted and spluttered alongside,
As the locals shared stories by the fireside.

Crane was shrewd and naïve (even if well read),
For stories of ghosts filled him with such dread.
Ichabod did not think himself to be daft,
Although he did believe in witchcraft.
The story that made the biggest impression,
Was the tale told of the galloping Hessian.
It was said the Hessian's ghost was to enslave,
Anyone who dared walk over his grave.
This made a lasting impression on Crane,
And would haunt him on down the lane.

On Sunday mornings, Ichabod led the chorus in song,
As pigeons bowed their heads, cooing all the daylong.
Within the church, music and voices filled the air,
'Twas at this time he beheld a lady, young and fair.
Now Ichabod Crane was known to be quite the charmer,
And it was here he took notice of the daughter of a rich farmer.
Katrina Van Tassel was a blooming plump lass,
Aside her family's wealth, she was held in high class.
With his soft heart, the foolish teacher was in a craze,
With dreams of great inheritance leaving him in a daze.

Crane pondered on where he might stand,
To try to win this rosy girl's hand.
This damsel, numerous lads did appraise,
For her fine assets held many to her gaze.
Ichabod knew there were many men to confront,
But none as burly than that of Brom Van Brunt.
A strong haughty man with a herculean frame,
His stout broad shoulders attracted many a dame.
Ichabod held his ground and did not forsake,
Even with Brom's bullying, he did not break.

Soon arrived from the Van Tassels homestead,
An invitation for merry making, drink, and bread.
An opportunity to see Katrina, what bliss!
A party Ichabod Crane was sure not to miss.
Oh, to dance with the lass, he would not dispute,
As Ichabod dawned his rusty black suit.
Sat astride a lean horse with a tangled tail,
The poor thing looked rather worn and frail.

When he arrived, such delight was well spent,
As he filled his stomach to his heart's content.
Merrily the guests became entranced;
The violin played a tune to which they danced.
Later, "Brom Bones" shared on that dance floor,
Legends of ghosts and spirits from old folklore.
Ichabod Crane tried not to be filled with such fright,
However, he could not shake the tales of that night.

Though Ichabod did not have Brom's stealth,
He was set to marry such procuring wealth.
So, as the evening settled, he set to aim,
A proposal to the prosperous young dame.
So did he dream to make her his bride,
But then Ichabod Crane was quickly denied.
It was then he hastily made his depart,
With heavy disappointment weighing on his heart.

As Ichabod strode along the dark trail,
His thoughts landed on that evening's ghost tale.
Never did the schoolteacher feel more alone,
As the wind gave out a howling moan.
Soon his imagination started to take flight,
As a mysterious cloaked rider came into sight.
"Who are you?" Ichabod gave with a cry,
But the shadowy guise gave no reply.

The massive figure fell into place,
Following aside Ichabod's same pace.
Uneasy, Ichabod kicked his poor steed,
In hopes to hasten his slow speed.
What he perceived, looking astride,
Made him rigid and most petrified.
For the pursuer's shoulders laid bare,
For he saw nothing resided there.

Along his saddle was strapped the head,
And into motion, Ichabod quickly fled.
Down the path he made his way,
Across the bridge where the church lay.
Looking back, he saw the stranger take chase,
And hurl his severed head at Ichabod's face.
Down he fell, into the dust and dark,
The shadowy rider having left his mark.

The next morning Ichabod was nowhere to be found.
Only his hat and a shattered pumpkin lay on the ground.
The lanky schoolteacher had vanished from sight,
And legend arose to what might have happened that night.
Gossip spread of spirits having taken him that day.
Others said it was the Hessian who carried him away.
No one knows for sure what occurred,
Or what Ichabod Crane must have endured.

As for Brom Bones, when the story was told,
Always smirked as if there was a secret to behold.
Having acted like someone exceedingly knowing;
Upon hearing the tale, his laughter was ongoing.
Such a man was he who never did falter,
Soon lead Katrina Van Tassel to the alter.
So comes the story of Ichabod Crane to an end,
That became known as the Sleepy Hollow legend.

# Bibliography


Algren, Nelson. "History and Legends of Popcorn, Cracker Jacks and Popcorn Balls." What's Cooking America. Original article from American Eats, published by University of Iowa Press, 1992, https://whatscookingamerica.net/history/popcornhistory.htm.

Barbezat, Suzanne. "Day of the Dead in Mexico: The CompleteGuide." TripSavvy, July 2, 2022, https://www.tripsavvy.com/day-of-the-dead-in-mexico-1588764.

Bhagat, Dhruti. "The Origins and Practices of: Samhain, Dia de los Muertos, and All Saints Day." Boston Public Library, Oct. 30,2018,https://www.bpl.org/blogs/post/the-origins-and-practices-of-holidays-samhain-dia-de-los-muertos-and-all-saints-day/ .

Bolinger, Hope. "The Dark Origin and History of Halloween." Crosswalk.com, Oct. 8. 2020, https://www.crosswalk.com/special-coverage/halloween/what-is-the-origin-and-history-of-halloween.html.

Bos, Brittney Anne. "The Strange History of the Ouija Board "What should we ask?"."The Haunted Walk, https://hauntedwalk.com/news/the-strange-history-of-the-ouija-board/. Accessed On Nov 22, 2022.

Buehner, Ted. "The Mysterious History of Halloween." MYNorthwest, Oct, 28, 2022, https://mynorthwest.com/3686302/mysterious-history-halloween/ .

Carlson, Laurie Winn. A Fever in Salem: A New Interpretation of the New England Witch Trials. Chicago, Ivan R. Dee, 1999.

Chewy Editorial. "Black Cats Throughout History." Bechewy, Sept. 1, 2022, https://be.chewy.com/black-cat-breeds-and-history/.

Colagrossi, Mike. "Halloween history: the ancient origins of these dark tradtions." Digital Media Center, Oct. 30, 2018, https://mycvdmc.org/2018/10/31/halloween-history-the-ancient-origins-of-these-dark-traditions/.

Coughlin, Sara. "Cauldrons, Broomsticks & Pointy Hats-A Real Witch
Explains These Common Symbols." Refinery 29, Oct 29, 2019,
https://www.refinery29.com/en-us/witch-symbols-broomstick-
cauldron-history-meaning.

Cybulskie, Daniele. "Memento Mori: Medieval Images of Death."
Medievalists.net,https://www.medievalists.net/2014/10/memento-mori-
medieval-images-death/. Accessed Nov. 3, 2022.

Formichella, Janice. "The unexpected romantic history of bobbing for
apples." Recollections, Oct. 10, 2021,https://recollections.biz/blog/the-
unexpected-romantic-history-of-bobbing-for-apples/.

Garrison, Greg. "Days of the Dead: What's the difference between All
Saints' and All Souls'?" Al.com, Nov. 1, 2013,https://www.al.com/living/
2013/11/days_of_the_dead_whats_the_dif.html.

Ghost, Davids. "History of Popcorn Balls, Recipes and Memories."
Hauntingly Good and Vintage Recipes from Long Ago, Oct. 18, 2015,
http://dddavidsvintagerecipes.blogspot.com/2015/10/history-of-popcorn-
balls-recipes-and.html.

Heller, Chris. "The History of the Haunted House." Smithsonian Magazine,
Oct. 28, 2015, updated Oct. 31, 2017, https://www.smithsonianmag.com/
history/history-haunted-house-180957008/.ß

History.com Editors. "Halloween 2022." History, last updated oct. 31, 2022,
https://www.history.com/topics/halloween/history-of-halloween.

History.com Editors. "How Trick or Treating Became a Halloween
Tradition." History.com, Oct. 22, 2022, https://www.history.com/news/
halloween-trick-or-treating-origins.

Irving, Washington. The Legend of Sleepy Hollow. London, John Murray, 1820.

Jones, Meghan. "What are the Halloween Colors, and What Do They
Mean?" Reader's Digest, Aug. 23, 2022, https://www.rd.com/article/
halloween-colors-black-and-orange/.

Kinerk, Alice. "A Brief History of the Humble Scarecrow". Key Peninsula News, Sept. 1, 2018,https://keypennews.org/stories/a-brief-history-of-the-humble-scarecrow,2265.

Lander, AK. "The history of gravestones." AK Lander: Complete peace of mind, Aug. 24, 2015, https://www.aklander.co.uk/news/history-gravestones.

Lesch, Nathan. "Halloween's 2000-year-old history." The Observer, Nov. 1, 2019, https://observer.case.edu/halloweens-2000-year-old-history/.

Lewis, Danny. "The Ancient Origins of Apple Cider." Smithsonian Magazine, Dec. 8, 2016, https://www.smithsonianmag.com/smart-news/ancient-origins-apple-cider-180960662/.

Little, Becky. "The Great Depression Origins of Halloween Haunted Houses." History, Oct. 31, 2018, https://www.history.com/news/halloween-haunted-house-great-depression.

Lohnes, Kate. "How Rye Bread May Have Caused the Salem Witch Trials." Britannica, https://www.britannica.com/story/how-rye-bread-may-have-caused-the-salem-witch-trials. Accessed Oct 2022.

Marduk. "All Hallow's Eve." Graham Hancock, Oct 26, 2004, https://grahamhancock.com/phorum/read.php?1,170344,170507.

Mark, Joshua J. "History of Halloween." World History Encyclopedia, Oct. 21, 2019, https://www.worldhistory.org/article/1456/history-of-halloween/.

Mason, Jessica. "Weird, Winding History of the Witch Hat." The Mary Sue, Oct. 26, 2020, https://www.themarysue.com/the-history-of-the-witch-hat/.

McCabe, Lyndsay. "A look Into the Cauldron: The Story Behind Halloween Symbols and Folklore." Longisland.com, Oct. 5, 2014,https://www.longisland.com/articles/10-05-14/halloween-symbols-and-folklore.html.

Meals, Roy A. "A Brief History of the Creepiness of Human Bones." Literary Hub, Oct. 30, 2020,https://lithub.com/a-brief-history-of-the-creepiness-of-human-bones/.

Miller, Dan. "The History of the Corn Mazes." Points with a Crew, Oct. 3, 2019, https://www.pointswithacrew.com/the-history-of-corn-mazes/.

Morton, Lisa. Trick or Treat: A History of Halloween. London, Reaktion Books Ltd. 2012.

Muise, Peter. "Halloween Magic: Grab your Cabbage." New England Folklore, Oct 26, 2013, http://newenglandfolklore.blogspot.com/2013/10/halloween-magic-grab-your-cabbage.html.

N/A. "15 Halloween Symbols Explained." King Halloween: Celebrate all year long, https://kinghalloween.com/halloween-favorites/halloween-symbols-explained/. Accessed Nov. 2022.

N/A. "About the Holiday." Creative Arts Guild, http://www.creativeartsguild.org/events/annual-events/dia-de-los-muertos/about-the-holiday. Accessed Oct. 2022.

N/A. "Cabbage Night: Freaky Facts." Spook Eats: Food. Travel. Supernatural, Oct. 12, 2018, https://spookeats.com/2018/10/12/cabbage-night-freaky-facts/.

N/A. "Day of the Dead Bread." Copal: Mexican Folk Art Guide, https://www.mexican-folk-art-guide.com/day-of-the-dead-bread.html#.Y5kBwi1h29Y. Accessed Dec. 2, 2022.

N/A. "Day of the Dead." Villa del Palmar Cancun, https://www.villapalmarcancun.com/blog/news/day-of-the-dead. Accessed Nov. 2022.

N/A. "Dia de los Muertos and Pan de Muerto". Eating the World, Oct. 24 2012, https://eatingtheworld.net/2012/10/24/dia-de-los-muertos-and-pan-de-muerto/.

N/A. "Get lost! A brief history of the corn maze." Morning AgClips, Oct. 13, 2022, https://www.morningagclips.com/get-lost-a-brief-history-of-the-corn-maze/.

N/A. "Halloween History: Fortune Telling Games." New-York Historical Society: Museum & Library, Oct 11, 2013, https://www.nyhistory.org/blogs/halloween-history-fortune-telling-games.

N/A. "Jewish Hat". Wikipedia, Wikimedia Foundation, last modified 13 Dec. 2022, https://en.wikipedia.org/wiki/Jewish_hat.

N/A. "Origins of Black Cat Superstitions!" Animal Emergency & referral Center of Minnesota, https://aercmn.com/origins-of-black-cat-superstitions/. Accessed Feb. 2022.

N/A. "Pan de ánimas". Wikipedia, Wikimedia Foundation, last modified 28 July 2022,https://en.wikipedia.org/wiki/Pan_de_ánimas.

N/A. "Pan De Muerto". Wikipedia, Wikimedia Foundation, last modified 1 Nov. 2022, https://en.wikipedia.org/wiki/Pan_de_muerto.

N/A. "Proctor's Ledge Memorial." 1692 Salem Witch Museum, https://salemwitchmuseum.com/locations/proctors-ledge-memorial/. Accessed Nov. 6, 2022.

N/A. "Salem witch trials". Wikipedia, Wikimedia Foundation, last modified 15 Dec, 2022, https://en.wikipedia.org/wiki/Salem_witch_trials.

N/A. "Samhain." Wikipedia, Wikimedia Foundation, last modified 20 Nov. 2022, https://en.wikipedia.org/wiki/Samhain.

N/A. "Stingy Jack." Wikipedia, Wikimedia Foundation, last modified 2 of Nov 2022, https://en.wikipedia.org/wiki/Stingy_Jack.

N/A. "Tarot". Wikipedia, Wikimedia Foundation, last modified 13 Dec. 2022, https://en.wikipedia.org/wiki/Tarot.

N/A. "The Legend of Stingy Jack." Old Soul Artisan, Oct. 8, 2018, https://oldsoulartisan.com/blogs/library/the-legend-of-stingy-jack.

N/A. "The Puritan Religion and How it Influenced the Salem Witch Trials." Ukessays, Aug. 12, 2021, https://www.ukessays.com/essays/history/influence-of-the-puritan-religion-on-the-salem-witch-trials.php.

N/A. "The Salem Witchcraft Papers." Salem Witch Trials: Documentary Archive and Transcription Project, Digital format 2018, https://salem.lib.virginia.edu/n59.html.

N/A. "The Wise Scarecrow of Japan and the origin of Scarecrow Festivals,
Rituals and Legends." Japanese Mythology & Folklore, Feb. 16, 2014,
https://japanesemythology.wordpress.com/2014/02/16/the-wise-scarecrow-
of-japan-and-the-origin-of-scarecrow-festivals-rituals-and-legends/.

N/A. "This is everything you need to know about the history of Halloween."
Pennlive, Oct.28, 2017, https://www.pennlive.com/opinion/2017/10/this_
is_everything_you_need_to.html.

N/A. "What is pan de muerto and why are Mexicans so crazy about it".
Hoteles City, https://www.cityexpress.com/en/travel-blog/pan-de-muerto-
and-why-are-mexicans-so-crazy-about-it. Accessed Nov. 27, 2022.

N/A. "Why Do we Bob for Apples on Halloween?" Irish Myths, Oct 12,
2022, https://irishmyths.com/2022/10/12/bobbing-for-apples/.

N/A. "Witch Hat". Wikipedia, Wikimedia Foundation, last modified 3
Nov. 2022, https://en.wikipedia.org/wiki/Witch_hat.

Olver, Lynne. "Halloween food traditions." The Food Timeline, 2005,
https://www.foodtimeline.org/halloween.html.

Prokop, Jessica. "The Surprising History of Candy Corn." CandyFavorites.com,
Oct. 12, 2012,  https://www.candyfavorites.com/blog/candy-corn-history/.

Reader's Staff. "Day of the Dead: The Art of Remembrance, September 21
through December 8." River Cities Reader, 10 Sept. 2019,
https://www.rcreader.com/art/day-dead-art-rememberance-sept21-dec8.

Robinson Robards, Julie. "Cabbage Night pranks have long history."
Press-Republican, Oct. 25, 2008, https://www.pressrepublican.com/news/
lifestyles/cabbage-night-pranks-have-long-history/article_e2306466-6888-
5fcb-8938-00e63e3d29bd.html.

Shanna. "Souling and Guising: The History of Trick or Treat." Luminous Lore,
Oct. 30, 2020, http://www.luminous-lore.com/halloween-trick-or-treat/.

Traverso, Vittoria. "In China, Ghosts Demanded the Finer Things in Life." Atlas Obscura, Oct. 19, 2017,https://www.atlasobscura.com/articles/china-ghost-festival-burning-money.

Wahl, Madeline. "Why Do We Bob for Apples on Halloween?" Reader's Digest, updated Oct. 31, 2022, https://www.rd.com/article/bobbing-for-apples/.

Weir, Laurie. "The ghoulish history of graveyards may haunt you." Simcoe.com, Oct 25, 2021, https://www.simcoe.com/news-story/10504737-the-ghoulish-history-of-graveyards-may-haunt-you/.

Weiss Simins, Jill. "Devil Cats, Magic Mirrors, and Fortune-Telling Cabbage: 19th Century Love-sick Hoosiers and Ancient Halloween Traditions." Hoosier State Chronicles, Oct. 27, 2016, https://blog.newspapers.library.in.gov/halloween2016/.

Wigington, Patti. "Scarecrow Folklore and Magic." Learn Religions, Aug. 18, 2018,https://www.learnreligions.com/scarecrows-guardians-of-the-harvest-2562307.

Wigle, Reda. "Day of the Dead 2022: The History and meaning behind the Mexican holiday." New York Post, Nov. 1, 2022, https://nypost.com/article/day-of-the-dead-history-meaning-explained/.

Yuko, Elizabeth. "Why Black Cats are Associated with Halloween and Bad Luck." History, Oct. 13, 2021,https://www.history.com/news/black-cats-superstitions.

Zito, Barbara Bellesi. "Halloween Colors: History and Meaning Behind Orange, Black, Purple and Green." Yahoo! Oct. 24, 2022,  https://www.yahoo.com/video/halloween-colors-history-meaning-behind-184149814.html.

Zoo, Mary. "Danse Macabre." Band Camp, https://maryzoo.bandcamp.com/track/danse-macabre. Accessed Nov. 2022.

# A Merry Hallowe'en

The End